MEDITATION

An Hachette UK Company
www.hachette.co.uk

First published in Great Britain in 2019 by Pyramid,
an imprint of Octopus Publishing Group Ltd
Carmelite House, 50 Victoria Embankment,
London EC4Y 0DZ
www.octopusbooks.co.uk

ISBN 978-0-7537-3350-9

A CIP catalogue record for this book is available from the
British Library

Printed and bound in China

10 9 8 7 6 5 4 3 2 1

Publisher: Lucy Pessell
Designer: Lisa Layton
Editor: Sarah Vaughan
Image credit: Pamela Nhlengethwa/Unsplash

Some of this material was previously published in *Working with
Meditation* and *The Meditation Bible* by Madonna Gauding.

MEDITATION

INTRODUCTION

If you are new to meditation, you will feel comfortable with this book. And if you are an experienced meditator, you may find renewed inspiration here. Whether you are a beginner or have been meditating for some time, this little book offers a collection of simple, effective meditations and words of inspiration to enrich your daily life and deepen your spiritual practice.

THROUGHOUT ITS LONG HISTORY, MEDITATION HAS BEEN ASSOCIATED WITH SPIRITUAL DEVELOPMENT

CALMING THE
MIND WAS NOT
A GOAL IN ITSELF;
RATHER, MEDITATION
PROVIDED A BASE FOR
SPIRITUAL ENQUIRY
AND PERSONAL
REALISATION; NOW
ATTAINABLE FOR ALL IN
VARIOUS CAPACITIES

THE BENEFITS
OF MEDITATION

Meditation has been practiced in many cultures for thousands of years because its benefits are numerous, as detailed on the next page. In all areas – physical, mental, emotional, psychological and spiritual – meditation has the potential to help you create a better life.

Better health – Simply meditating on your breath can lower your blood pressure, slow your heart rate and ease anxiety.

Sharpen your mind – You can bring your new found mental skill and discipline to your work and family life.

Boost awareness of your body and mind – Improve your concentration and feel less overloaded with life.

Balance the emotions – Stay conscious of your emotions and help create mental peace and less emotional reactivity.

Heal psychological problems – If you have suffered from addictions, grief, trauma or other psychological issues, meditation is a wonderful way to support yourself during the healing process.

Contemplate the mysteries of life – If you feel bogged down in the materialistic view of the world that pervades our culture, meditate to transform and transcend it.

Help understand the meaning of life – Meditation will aid your connection to your destiny, connectedness to all living being and the sacredness of reality.

You may think that meditation is an exotic practice which is connected with Eastern religions. Or you may think it has something to do with a special sitting posture. You may also think it has to do with being 'holy'. This may be where it began but today's practice is attainable for all.

MEDITATION IS SIMPLY MAKING A CHOICE TO FOCUS YOUR MIND ON SOMETHING – READING A BOOK IS A FORM OF MEDITATION, AS IS WATCHING A MOVIE OR PREPARING A MEAL

Meditation is not mystical, otherworldly or inaccessible. It is not reserved for the 'elite' nor those steeped in knowledge of Eastern or alternative religions. Meditation is very down-to-earth and practical and it is available to everyone. Although many of the meditations in this book are inspired by ancient and modern spiritual traditions, none requires faith or belief. If you have no spiritual practice, or do not believe in a god or higher power, be inspired and try these meditations with the motivation of simply creating a happier life for yourself.

This little book will help you make space and time in any day for meditating and focusing your mind in positive and helpful ways.

MEDITATION IS THE KEY TO THE MIND

Our everyday lives are like a waking dream. Rather than being truly awake and aware, we are usually preoccupied or lost in thought. One thought triggers another – and another and another. Buddhists affectionately call this ordinary state of mind 'monkey mind', as if our minds were filled with unruly chimps leaping from branch to branch. We may start with one thought and end up with another that is entirely unrelated to the first. Our thoughts seem to have a life of their own.

The purpose of examining our normal mental state is not so that we can judge ourselves; after all, every person on the planet can relate to these ordinary states of mind. But, as we will discover, the mind is capable of much more, and meditation is a key to its unfolding.

MEDITATION HAS THE POTENTIAL TO DEEPEN OUR UNDERSTANDING OF THE GREATER MYSTERIES OF LIFE

HOW TO START

START WITH AN OPEN MIND

If you are new to meditation, you may find your views challenged by some of the exercises. If you are an experienced meditator, you may find the meditations are different from those you are used to.

FOUR WAYS TO MEDITATE:

1.   Learning to focus and concentrate. By training the mind to focus on an object such as a candle or an image, on the breath itself or even on a movement such as walking, you become aware of your normal uncontrolled thinking patterns and eventually learn to quiet your mind.

2.   Learning about yourself, and the world around you, without the filters of unbalanced emotion, fantasy or projection. This is sometimes called mindfulness, insight or awareness meditation.

3.   Contemplate a topic. The early Christians meditated on passages of the New Testament. Tibetan Buddhists practice 'analytical meditation' on topics such as compassion, patience and generosity.

4.   Engage the mind's ability to imagine or visualize, to help you create the mind and reality you want.

WHAT YOU'LL NEED

Although they are not essential, there are a few items that you may want to invest in to make your meditation more comfortable and productive. You will need:

- Cushion or chair
- Mats
- Blankets and shawls
- Loose clothing

IN THE BEGINNING, YOU MAY HAVE TROUBLE STAYING WITH A DAILY DISCIPLINE DUE TO THE PRESSURES OF LIFE. BUT COMMITTING TO A DAILY PRACTICE IS THE BEST WAY TO APPROACH MEDITATION

CREATE A SACRED
SPACE IN WHICH YOU
CAN CONNECT WITH
A WORLD BEYOND
YOUR ORDINARY,
EVERYDAY ONE

BE WILLING TO LET
MEDITATION CHANGE
YOU. EVEN IF IT IS
POSITIVE, CHANGE
CAN BE SCARY.
BUT THE BENEFITS
FAR OUTWEIGH
THE TEMPORARY
DISCOMFORT THAT
COMES WITH CHANGE

CONCENTRATION MEDITATION ON THE BREATH

Meditating or concentrating on the breath, on a daily basis, provides a solid foundation for all other forms of meditation. Ancient Hindus and Buddhists meditated in this way to tame uncontrolled thinking and reduce negative thoughts and actions, as a way to prepare their minds to be receptive to spiritual truths. Basically, you meditate on your breath in order to give your mind something to 'hang on to' when it starts to jump from one thought to another. Training your mind in this way helps you focus on one thing at a time and develop your powers of concentration. It has a calming influence on your body and mind, and is beneficial for reducing negativity and anxiety, as well as lowering the heart rate and blood pressure.

1. Sit cross-legged on a cushion, with your buttocks slightly raised (if you can't sit cross-legged, sit on a chair). Keep your back straight, your shoulders level and relaxed and your chin parallel to the floor. Lower your eyes and focus about one metre (three feet) in front of you. Rest your hands gently on your knees.

2. Breathe normally through your nose, using your abdomen rather than your chest. Check your posture, and relax any part of your body that is tense.

3. Begin counting your breath on each exhalation, and when you reach ten, begin again. Thoughts will intervene and, when they do, simply let them go and return to counting your breath.

4. After ten minutes or so, end the session. Try to bring focus and concentration into your daily life.

THE CLASSICAL SEVEN-POINT POSTURE

Although you may not be able to master the classical seven-point posture right away, it is worth the effort to try and do so. If it seems impossible, do the best you can. If nothing else, keep your spine straight. Correct posture helps your mind find peace, strength and control. It benefits your physical body by bringing your energies and body systems into balance.

1.   Sit on the floor, with your back – from the nape of your neck to the small of your back – as straight as possible. Imagine a pile of coins stacked on top of one another.

2.   Cross your legs. Your right leg should be above your left leg and the backs of your feet should sit flat on the tops of your knees. Your two feet should make a straight line.

3.   Your shoulders should be even and relaxed. Try not to sit with one shoulder higher than the other.

4.   Your chin should be level with the floor, and tucked in slightly.

5.   Your eyes should be relaxed, open and slightly lowered, looking into space, at nothing in particular, somewhere about one metre (three feet) in front of you.

6.   Your tongue should be placed against your upper palate.

7.   Your lips should be slightly parted, and your teeth should be touching, but not clenched. Breathe through your nose.

MINDFULNESS MEDITATION

When you are awake, your mind jumps from one thought to another, like a monkey leaping from branch to branch. You may have had the experience of driving to the supermarket, getting lost in thought and 'waking up' as you pull into the car park. During the drive you probably had hundreds of thoughts, and countless images and impressions crossing your mind. It was as if the car was on automatic and drove itself to the shop.

THIS MEDITATION IS DESIGNED TO HELP YOU OBSERVE YOUR MIND AND ITS TENDENCY TO JUMP FROM ONE THOUGHT TO ANOTHER

1. Sit in your meditation posture on a chair or cushion and take a few deep breaths.

2. Begin to observe your thoughts. Notice how quickly and seamlessly your mind jumps from one idea, impression or thought to another. Think back a few minutes ago and try to remember what you were thinking. Trace how you got to what you are thinking at the moment.

3. Look at a watch or a clock in order to time yourself, and for the next 60 seconds, make hash marks with a pencil on some paper every time your thoughts change during that minute.

4. Bring this new awareness of 'monkey mind' into your daily life. Try to be more mindful of what you are thinking, rather than getting lost in thought.

RATHER THAN BEING
AWAKE TO REALITY
AS IT IS, AND TRULY
AWARE OF WHAT IS
GOING ON AROUND
AND INSIDE US, IT IS
AS IF WE ARE LIVING
IN A DREAM WORLD –
A SMALL, CONFINING
WORLD OF OUR MIND'S
CREATION…

MEDITATION HELPS US TO FOCUS AND 'WAKE UP'; TO WELCOME THAT WHICH WE TRULY NEED, OR LET GO OF WHAT WE DO NOT

MEDITATIONS FOR BODY, MIND & SPIRIT

YOU HAVE A BODY

Meditating on mindfulness of physical sensations allows you to become more aware of your body, if you feel like you need to reconnect with your physical self.

TRY THIS MINDFULNESS MEDITATION WHENEVER YOU ARE FEELING DISCONNECTED FROM YOUR BODY

1. Sit on a cushion or a chair keeping your back as straight as possible, yet relaxed. Calm your mind by observing your breath.

2. Shift the focus on your breath to another part of your body. Choose a spot that is easy to feel, like your neck or your knee. Focus all your awareness on that spot. Try to merge with any sensations you may feel. Observe the sensation without judging it as pleasant or unpleasant.

3. Is the sensation a tightness, a burning or a tingling? Is it a combination of many sensations? Do they change over time? Keep your awareness on the spot. If thoughts intrude, return your focus to the spot you have chosen.

4. If you want, switch to another part of your body and repeat the same exercise. When ready, end your meditation. Try to bring this mindfulness of your body into your daily life.

YOGA AND MEDITATION

The original goal of the ancient practice of yoga was spiritual transformation. When you bring meditation to your practice of simple yoga poses, as described on pages 37–39, this will not only give you a healthier body, but will help you change your mental habits, your attitudes and your outlook on life. It will assist you in expanding your consciousness and will put you in touch with your deeper wisdom.

TRY THIS POSE WHENEVER YOU NEED TO CLEAR YOUR MIND

CHILD POSE

1.   Kneel on the floor and sit back with your feet together and your buttocks resting on your heels. (If you have difficulty doing this, place a folded towel or blanket between your thighs and calves.) Separate your knees by about the width of your hips. Place your hands on your thighs, palms down.

2.   Inhale deeply, then exhale as you fold yourself forwards, place your chest to rest between your thighs and rest your forehead on the floor. Bring your arms around to your sides until your hands are resting on either side of your feet, relaxed, with the palms up and fingers slightly curled. Release any tension in your shoulders and let them fall towards the floor, naturally opening the space between your shoulder blades.

3.   Breathe gently through your nose and feel your breath expanding into the back of your torso, as it lengthens and widens your spine. Let go and relax completely.

SUN SALUTATION

This famous yoga *asana*, *surya-namaskar*, will get you moving early in the day and give you a sense of gratitude and purpose.

PRACTISE THIS AS AN AWAKENING MEDITATION FIRST THING IN THE MORNING

1.	Stand with your feet hip-width apart, hands by your sides. Inhale, raise your arms overhead and arch back as far as feels comfortable.

2.	As you exhale, bend forward and rest your hands beside your feet. Inhale and step the right leg back with hands still on the floor.

3.	Exhale and step the left leg back. Now you are in a push-up position with arms fully extended. Hold the position and inhale. Exhale and lower yourself as if coming down from a push-up. Only your hands and feet should touch the floor.

4.	Inhale and stretch forward and up, bending at the waist. Use your arms to lift your torso, but only bend back as far as is comfortable. Exhale, lift and push your hips back and up with your head facing down between your straight legs.

5.	Inhale and step your right foot forward. Exhale, bring your left foot forward and pull your head to your knees. Inhale and stand tall while keeping your arms extended over your head. Exhale and lower your arms to your sides. Repeat the sequence, stepping back with the left leg first.

WALKING ZEN

Zen Buddhists practice a wonderful walking meditation called *kinhin*. You do not have to be a Buddhist to enjoy this calming, centring, mindful and moving meditation.

TRY THIS WHEN YOU WANT TO SLOW DOWN AND BE MORE PRECISE IN YOUR WORK OR YOUR RELATIONSHIPS

1.   Mark out a route beforehand. You can do walking meditation indoors by circling around a room or by walking outdoors in your garden or along a path. If outdoors, it should be where you can be alone.

2.   Stand with your back straight and try to remain relaxed. Place your hands together just below your sternum or heart, with your left hand in a soft fist, wrapping your fingers lightly around your thumb. Then place your right hand over your left with your right thumb across the top of your left hand. Keep your elbows slightly extended from your sides.

3.   Begin walking slowly along the route you decided on in your preparation, either inside or outside. Begin by taking a half-step with every cycle of breath (inhalation and exhalation). So, it is heel first (half-step) and ball of foot (half-step). Your pace will be extremely slow. As you walk, focus on your breath. Keep your eyes lowered and directed straight ahead. Don't look from side to side.

4.   Stop. Now switch to a normal walking pace for a few minutes. Keep focusing on your breath. Breathe naturally. End your meditation when you feel ready to do so.

MEDITATION ON FINDING YOUR TRUE SELF

Meditation can benefit us in many ways, one of which can be coming to the understanding of who we really are.

ANY TIME YOU ARE FEELING
STRESSED AND HEMMED
IN BY WORRIES ABOUT
YOUR IDENTITY, USE THIS
MEDITATION

1.   Sit in the meditation posture for five minutes. Think for a minute of the different personas you present to different people. Do you behave inconsistently in front of your boss, your friends, your spouse, strangers? Become a few of these many personas in your mind by imagining that you are having conversations with different people in your life. What aspect of yourself are you putting forward with each one? Do not judge yourself, or feel that you are being false. We all present different aspects of our personality in different situations.

2.   Now try to imagine your essential self, your best self, the one who is without artifice or neurosis. Imagine that you are free of any negativities or delusions, and that you are filled with love and compassion for all beings. Imagine that you possess complete wisdom and knowledge. Imagine that you are enlightened.

3.   Imagine that you have reached your more authentic, loving, compassionate self. Think about a different quality with each breath. Meditate on your true self for as long as you desire.

RUNNER'S WAY

If you are a runner, you may have already experienced a meditative state while running. As a practice, running alone can be a great way to regain personal focus.

USE THIS MEDITATION TO MAKE YOUR TIME RUNNING MORE FOCUSED AND CONSCIOUS

1. Begin meditating as you put on your T-shirt, shorts and running shoes. Do this mindfully, focusing on each task.

2. As you begin running, meditate by watching your breath, except you are moving instead of sitting down on a cushion or chair.

3. Now let go of your concentration on your breath, and focus on the act of running. Try not to let thoughts enter your mind; when they do, simply return your focus to running. Begin to feel your body, mind and soul functioning together as one. Continue to stay in the present moment, very much aware of everything around you.

4. When you finish your run, take off your shoes and socks and stand on the grass. Feel connected to the Earth and grounded in your body. Continue to be mindful of the present throughout your day.

NATURE SOOTHES, NATURE HEALS

Beauty and wisdom await you in a fragrant pine wood, on a deserted beach, by a still pond or a flowing stream. If you don't have time to get out into the wild in order to meditate, then simply meditating in the nearest park or in your own back garden will do.

WHEN YOU MEDITATE IN NATURE, MENTALLY CREATE A SACRED SPACE AROUND YOU

MANY OF US WHO LIVE
IN CITIES AND SPEND
MOST OF OUR LIVES
INDOORS HAVE LOST
OUR CONNECTION TO
THE NATURAL WORLD.
MEDITATION HELPS YOU
RECONNECT WITH
NATURE AND ALLOW
YOUR SPIRIT TO FEEL A
PART OF THE WORLD
AROUND YOU

MEDITATION ON CLOUDS

Pick a day when the sky is blue and the clouds are white and plentiful. Not only will this meditation help you reconnect with the nature around you but it will elevate your thoughts up towards the sky and let your body feel the elements.

TRY THIS MEDITATION WHEN NEGATIVE THOUGHTS OR EMOTIONS ARISE

1. Find a place outdoors where you can see the clouds in the sky. If you like, lie down on the grass for a better view.

2. Take in the feeling of looking up into the vastness above. If you are like most people, you may actually forget to look up at the sky for days or weeks on end. You know it's there, but your eyes are mostly focused (indoors or out) straight ahead.

3. Breathe deeply for a moment and note to yourself how this feels. What thoughts come to mind?

4. Notice how the clouds move and change. Whether moving fast or slowly, they are in constant flux. They do not stay the same from one second to the next. Realize that you are like the clouds. You too are not the same from one moment to the next. Nothing is fixed or static, in you or in nature.

5. Contemplate this idea and let your thoughts and emotions emerge and disappear like the clouds above you. Why cling to them?

MEDITATION ON A LEAF

To perceive without bias or judgement is a difficult task for anyone. Unfortunately, labelling and judgements prevent you from experiencing life directly. This simple awareness meditation will help you to experience nature more deeply and joyfully.

PRACTISE THIS MEDITATION WHEN YOU FEEL SEPARATED FROM NATURE AND DISTANCED FROM YOUR OWN DIRECT EXPERIENCE OF LIFE

1.   Walk for a few minutes in the park or woods while focusing on your breath. Try to empty your mind of all thoughts.

2.   Stop walking, pick up a fallen leaf and hold it in your hand. Notice if you are judging the leaf in any way – for its appearance, size or colour, or if you are comparing it to another you didn't pick up. Try to let go of any thoughts or judgements about the leaf.

3.   Begin by simply taking in the leaf visually as if you were a Martian and had never seen one before. Notice its exquisite shape, colour and the tiny delicate veins spreading from its centre. If it has blemishes from insects or decay, see them as equally beautiful and perfect.

4.   Spend time being with the leaf in this way. Try to bring this way of experiencing the leaf to the rest of your life. Notice if you feel more relaxed, more fulfilled and more aware of the beauty all around you.

MEDITATION
ON FLOWERS

Flowers offer one of the most stunning displays of nature, and the best way to enjoy them is outdoors in a garden setting. It is here – in the company of insects, the sun, the rain and the earth – that you can best experience the overwhelming, and sometimes breathtaking, beauty of nature

1. Sit or stand in front of flowers that attract you. Close your eyes, breathe deeply and take in their perfume.

2. Open your eyes and let their form and colour flood your vision. Notice any insects buzzing around them – perhaps a bee or a butterfly. Try not to think about the flowers; just let them enter and permeate your consciousness. Are you smiling?

MEDITATION ON FIRE

Meditation on an external object builds focus and concentration. One of the best objects for meditation is fire or a flame. It can be a candle, a fire in your fireplace or an outdoor bonfire. As humans we naturally gravitate towards fire and have a fascination for it – perhaps because it is primal and essential for our existence.

1. Seat yourself near a candle flame or fire, either on a cushion in traditional meditation posture or on a chair with your feet flat on the ground and your spine straight. Close your eyes and take three deep breaths. Now open your eyes and focus on the flame or fire. Try not to let thoughts or emotions intrude. When they do, simply return to gazing single-mindedly at the flame or fire.

2. Meditate for a minimum of ten minutes. If possible, do this on a daily basis for one month and notice how it affects your ability to focus.

MEDITATIONS FOR LOVE & COMPASSION

Self-hatred is common in our culture, including the acceptance of shame we place on ourselves or unintentionally upon others. The following meditations will help you counteract any feelings of self-hatred, including low self-esteem, and help you to develop love, joy, self-respect and well-being towards yourself as well as for others.

THE MANY CHANGES,
REALIZATIONS AND
BENEFITS OF MEDITATION
CAN ACCUMULATE
OVER TIME. THERE IS NO
QUICK FIX OR INSTANT
ENLIGHTENMENT. THAT
IS NOT TO SAY THAT
MEDITATION WILL NOT
FEEL GOOD RIGHT
AWAY, BUT REGULAR
PRACTICE WILL REAP
BIGGER REWARDS

LOVE YOURSELF

Some may argue that the best place to start in your medative journey towards love and compassion is to begin with directing that love towards yourself.

TRY THIS MEDITATION WHEN YOU BECOME AWARE OF SELF-HATRED AND WISH TO FEEL SELF-LOVE AGAIN

1.	Sit on a cushion or chair in a quiet place. Visualize your higher power sitting in front of you. It could be Jesus, Buddha, Shakti, Mohammed or just a wise form of your self.

2.	Imagine your higher power smiling at you with great love and compassion, accepting you as you are. Understand that he or she does not demand that you 'fix' anything about yourself to deserve his or her love. Know that he or she wants you to accept yourself exactly as you are, and treat yourself with kindness and respect as they already do.

3.	Thank your higher power for reminding you to be kind towards yourself. Tell him or her that with their help and encouragement, you will refrain from hating yourself and will encourage yourself to accept yourself exactly as you are. Promise that you will try to live your life with complete self-acceptance and self-love.

REPAYING KINDNESS

This is a wonderful meditation for realizing the kindness of others. It will help you develop compassion and reduce any self-centredness that may creep into your thoughts.

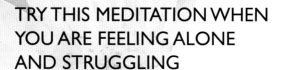

TRY THIS MEDITATION WHEN YOU ARE FEELING ALONE AND STRUGGLING

1.   Begin by making a list of everyone who took
        care of you as a child. Sit on your cushion
        or straight-backed chair. Light a candle in
        memory of all those who have helped you in
        your life.

2.   Recall the list you made in preparation for
        your meditation. Begin with your mother
        and father; then go on to siblings, aunts and
        uncles, grandparents and cousins, all of whom
        cared for you in some way. Then think of your
        teachers, your babysitters, clergy, coaches and
        friends. Think of your first job and the person
        who hired you. Now consider the farmers who
        grew the food you ate and the shops that sold
        the food. Return to your parents who worked
        hard for you to have a home, clothes, food,
        schooling and medical care. Think of your
        doctors and dentists. Your list is merely the tip
        of the iceberg.

3.   Continue to add to your list. Generate a sincere
        sense of gratitude to every person who has
        helped you in your life. Realize you have been
        the recipient of so much kindness it will take
        lifetimes to repay everyone. Vow to pay back
        all of that kindness by generating love and
        compassion for them and for all beings.

Having mental peace and less emotional reactivity are benefits of long-term meditation practice. Researchers have found that meditating on compassion, for example, can cause positive changes, over time, in a part of the brain known as the *amygdala* – the area involved in processing emotion.

In Buddhism, patience means 'forbearance' and refers to that quality of remaining calm in the face of adversity or provocation. Specifically, it means not giving in to your anger. Anger is a strong force within everyone. On a day-to-day level, notice how you can become irritated by the most trivial of things, despite your good nature.

THE BUDDHA
RECOMMENDED
DEALING WITH
ANGER THROUGH
MEDITATION, IN ORDER
TO BECOME CALMER,
MORE AWARE OF YOUR
EMOTIONS AND MORE
LOVING OF OTHERS

UNCONDITIONAL LOVE

Most often our love is conditional – based on whether our loved ones behave the way we would like or support us in our endeavours. But a better love is one without conditions – we love them as they are, regardless of what they do.

PRACTISE THIS MEDITATION IF YOU HAVE CONTROL ISSUES IN YOUR RELATIONSHIPS

1. Sit on a cushion or chair in your private meditation space. Begin by watching your breath and calming body and mind.

2. Bring to mind your partner or other loved one. List any conditions you have that limit your love for them. For example, you may find you love them on condition that they make a lot of money, buy you flowers for special events or wear certain clothes. Note how these conditions, while seeming rational, constrict your heart. Note how this doesn't sound like love, more like a demand that your needs be met.

3. Now visualize giving your loved one complete freedom to be and do what they want. Does this frighten you, make you sad or change how you feel about them? Bring to mind the qualities you love about this person. Perhaps you love their energy, their courage and their ability to respond to others.

4. Imagine them not being with you or available to meet your needs and loving them anyway. Feel your heart expand as you accept and love them wholeheartedly, regardless of what they do or don't do.

BROTHERS AND SISTERS

All religions encourage you to love your parents, but many do not say as much about siblings. By meditating on the relationship between you and your sibling (or a close friend you think of as a sibling) you may begin to see that relationship blossom, by encouraging love between you.

THIS IS A GREAT MEDITATION TO PRACTISE BEFORE MEETING UP, OR EVEN BEFORE HAVING A CONVERSATION

1. Sit on your cushion or chair in your meditation space. Place some photos of your siblings on a table in front of you. Light a candle. Meditate on your breath for a few minutes. Now call on your higher power to sit alongside you. Introduce him or her to your siblings.

2. Let any feelings emerge. Ask your higher power to help you heal your relationships, if they need healing. If they don't, ask that your relationships deepen and strengthen over your lifetimes. If you have unproductive ways of relating that are rooted in your childhood, ask that you be able to shed them and find a new, more mature model.

3. Now recall the positive qualities in each of your brothers and sisters. Ask that you be able to accept and love them exactly as they are.

4. Close your meditation by committing to honour and respect each of your siblings (or close friends) and strengthen the relationships you have with them.

Being able to give your full attention to your partner, child or sibling helps them feel respected or loved. By focusing on your love towards them through meditation, these feelings will develop in your heart, and them be revealed in your actions between each other.

IF YOU WANT TO
STAY CONSCIOUS
OF YOUR EMOTIONS
AND MONITOR YOUR
EMOTIONAL PATTERNS,
TRY MEDITATING TO
TRANSFORM NEGATIVE
EMOTIONS INTO
POSITIVE ONES

After you have explored the different forms of meditation and ways in which you can experience love and compassion, you may find one or two practices you want to stay with on a long-term basis. At this point, settle on a time and place that is consistent day to day.

SURRENDER YOUR BODY AND EMBRACE THE ART OF 'DOING NOTHING'

MEDITATIONS
FOR PROBLEM
SOLVING

WAKING UP TO REALITY

When something happens to jolt us out of our usual mental state – such as the loss of a job, the death of a loved one or a diagnosis of serious illness – we feel disoriented, life seems turned on its head and some parts of our nature, that we may not have known existed, are revealed. We may feel the need to control a situation, have trouble making a difficult decision or have trouble sleeping, all of which results in an imbalance in our lives.

Meditating upon specific, personal issues can help us understand our inner emotions and can provide us with the clarity we need to move forward and overcome.

What is at first a tragedy can sometimes be an opportunity for profound awakening, because our mind is jolted out of our normal 'dream state'. The good news is that rather than waiting for the world to shock us into awareness, we can choose to live in an awakened state all the time. Meditation is the antidote to living in a dream world. It is the conscious act of training the mind, through a variety of mental and physical techniques, so as to live fully in the present moment and address the problems that try to restrict us.

YOU CAN LET GO NOW

Do you have control issues? Has anyone told you that you are controlling? Meditating will help you learn to let go of the fears, doubts, worries and other emotions surrounding the need to be in control, or to control others.

IF YOU HAVE RECEIVED ANY COMPLAINTS ABOUT YOUR CONTROLLING BEHAVIOUR, YOU MIGHT WANT TO TRY THIS MEDITATION

1. Write about three occasions on which you can remember feeling anxiety and wanting to control someone else's behaviour, even if it seemed justified to you at the time. Sit on a cushion or chair in your meditation space. Watch your breath for five minutes.

2. Choose one of the events you listed. Try to recall it in detail. Feel what you were feeling at the time. Perhaps your partner moved a chair and didn't move it back to where you had placed it when he or she left the room. Was your first feeling one of anger?

3. Ask yourself why it is so important to have things the way you want them, especially since you are sharing your life with another person. If you weren't feeling anger, would you feel fear? Are you afraid something may happen unexpectedly and you will feel powerless, alone, abandoned? Explore the fear behind your need to control.

4. Commit to letting go a little at a time on a daily basis by looking for the fear behind the need for you to control. Relax your grip on things and notice that usually nothing terrible happens. Be kind and patient with yourself in this process.

HIGH ROAD

If you are facing a difficult decision, where 'doing the right thing' may have negative consequences, it may be hard to follow your moral and ethical principles. This meditation will help you take the 'high road' if that is what you choose to do.

TRY THIS MEDITATION TO
HELP YOU LIVE ACCORDING
TO YOUR VALUES

1.   Sit on a cushion or chair and meditate by watching your breath for five minutes.

2.   Bring to mind the situation that is troubling you. If there were no negative consequences, what would you do? What action would feel most congruent with your values? Visualize yourself talking to whomever you need to and taking any action you feel appropriate.

3.   Visualize the same situation, but this time bring to mind any negative consequences that may come your way if you do what you feel is right. Imagine how you will feel if you lost your job or your friend? Would you feel more comfortable if you acted in line with how you would like to live your life? Would acting on your principles help some and harm others?

4.   Sometimes there are no black or white answers, but spending time quietly trying out ethical decisions is the best way to come to know what is best. Ask your higher power to help you make the most compassionate decision for yourself and anyone else involved.

MAKE PEACE
WITH MONEY

Money – making it, having it, not having it, wanting it – is central to most people's lives and a source of great anxiety for many. But it isn't just money we find ourselves obsessing about. Materialism and the constant need for 'more' - more clothes, more 'things', better cars, a bigger home - can drag us down.

TRY THIS MEDITATION IF
YOU ARE WORRIED ABOUT
MATERIALISTIC TENDENCIES

1.   Write about what money means to you and what role it plays in your life. Sit on a cushion or straight-backed chair in your private meditation space. Breathe deeply for a few minutes to clear your mind.

2.   Review what you wrote down. Explore how you feel when you have money. Do you feel more real? Do you feel you exist more solidly than when you don't have money?

3.   Now imagine how you feel when you are broke. Are you diminished, deflated and less valuable? Notice you don't become more solid or less substantial when you have or don't have money. Contemplate how money functions as an idea.

4.   Contemplate ten things that are not measured in monetary terms, such as the loving gaze of your partner, a wonderful conversation with a friend, the laughter of your child or the playfulness of your pet.

4.   End your meditation by affirming that you are valuable with or without money. Commit to meditating on the meaning of money to help you counteract the message of materialism.

GET OUT OF DEBT

The habit of living beyond your means may be dragging you down mentally, physically and spiritually. This meditation will help you to find the courage to get yourself out of debt.

TRY THIS MEDITATION IF YOU NEED TO ADDRESS YOUR SPENDING OR LIFESTYLE HABITS

1.   Sit on a cushion or chair in your meditation space. Light a candle to help you focus.

2.   Gather your records together and add up how much you are in debt. Say the amount out loud: 'I am [however much] in debt'. Let that fact resonate in your consciousness. How do you feel saying that fact out loud? If you feel numb or if you feel fear, anxiety or shame, note it. How does your body feel when you say the amount out loud? Do you experience a feeling of tension or is your breathing constricted?

3.   After admitting to yourself the extent of your debt, generate a sense of compassion for your difficulties in controlling your spending. From this place of compassion commit to getting out of debt, no matter how long it takes. Ask your higher power to help you control your spending and give you the courage to seek professional help if you need it.

4   End your meditation by making a promise to your higher power that you will stop spending on credit and will reduce the amount you owe every month by paying off some of the balance.

WORKAHOLISM

What used to be called 'workaholism' is fast becoming the norm for many people. Long hours and taking work home is expected if you want to compete in the corporate world. This meditation helps you to find a better alternative.

TRY THIS MEDITATION IF
YOU ARE QUESTIONING
YOUR FAST-PACED OR
OVERWHELMING LIFESTYLE

1.   Start by writing down your typical schedule for a week. Sit on a cushion or chair in your meditation space. Meditate by watching your breath for five minutes.

2.   Look over your schedule. How much time did you spend with your loved ones or friends? Did you get eight hours' sleep a night? When did you relax and play during the week? Did you eat well and exercise? Did you tend to your spiritual life? Are you using your hectic schedule to avoid intimacy? How much money are you really making an hour?

3.   Now contemplate your long-term goals. What do you want to achieve? When you are on your deathbed, how and with who do you want to have spent your life?

4.   Think about the qualities you would like to manifest in your life. Do you want warmth, love, fun, play, spiritual development and time in nature? How is your current life helping you have this quality of life?

5.   End your meditation by affirming what is most important to you and committing to creating a more balanced life.

FACING THE MIRROR AND YOUR PROBLEMS FACE ON

Everyone has difficulties and problems that persist over time. You are not alone in this. Meditation can help you face your problems directly, with courage and honesty.

TRY THIS MEDITATION WHEN YOU FEEL YOU ARE AVOIDING YOUR PROBLEMS

1. Find a time when you can be alone. Stand in front of your bathroom mirror or a full-length mirror.

2. Look at your reflection. Speaking out loud, tell yourself three things you like about yourself. It could be that you are a good listener, a very intelligent person or a great cook. Love the person looking back at you. Tell yourself you know you are struggling, but it is important to admit to the problem that has been dragging you down.

3. Out loud, in a clear voice, tell yourself the problem you have been avoiding. For example, you might say 'I am overweight and I need to lose it for my health and well-being'. Repeat your statement three times.

4. Now commit to taking a step to resolve your problem within the next 24 hours. Say out loud what you plan to do. Repeat it three times.

5. Close your meditation by congratulating yourself for your courage and honesty.

MEDITATING ON BREATH

You meditate on your breath in order to give your mind something to 'hang on to' when it starts to jump from one thought to another. Training your mind in this way helps you focus on one thing at a time and develop your powers of concentration.

MEDITATING OR
CONCENTRATING ON
THE BREATH, ON A
DAILY BASIS, PROVIDES
A SOLID FOUNDATION
FOR ALL OTHER FORMS
OF MEDITATION

GETTING TO SLEEP

There is a large number of people who find it distressingly difficult to get to sleep easily, but help is at hand if you choose to apply meditation to your daily life, or make tiny changes to your bedtime routine.

THE FOLLOWING FOUR CONSIDERATIONS MAY HELP YOU TO MAKE A RELAXED TRANSITION FROM THE WORLD OF OBJECTS TO DEEP SLEEP

1.   Limit your intake of stimulants such as caffeine, tobacco and sugar, especially shortly before going to bed.

2.   Avoid eating a heavy meal for at least two hours before bedtime. Instead, choose easily digestible, nutritious foods. Some foods, for example bananas and lettuce, are recommended as having sleep-inducing properties.

3.   In bed, posture is important. Relax your whole body into the mattress. Lie there mindfully, quietly maximising the sense of rest. Consider also the direction you sleep in and the kind of mattress you use. Experiment. See what works so that you can enter the channel from the waking state through the dream world into deep sleep on Earth.

4.   The greatest contribution to a good night's sleep is a relaxed attitude towards events during the day – a mindful attitude during the day can contribute greatly.

BEGINNING
A PROJECT OR
FULFILLING A
DREAM

You may want to manifest your dreams, but fear may be holding you back. Try this meditation to help you take the leap and make your vision a reality.

TRY THIS MEDITATION IF YOU
FEEL READY TO MANIFEST
A DREAM, BUT ARE AFRAID
TO MOVE FORWARD,
OR FIND YOURSELF
PROCRASTINATING

1. Sit on a cushion or chair in your meditation space. Meditate by watching your breath for five minutes.

2. Bring to mind a dream you would like to manifest. Ask yourself why you have not moved forward to make it a reality. Explore your beliefs about yourself and how they may be getting in your way.

3. For example, if you have always wanted to learn to ride a horse but are afraid of getting hurt or you feel it is too extravagant for your lifestyle or more fun than you deserve, then examine those beliefs and counter them with new ones. As an example, tell yourself millions of people ride horses without getting hurt, it is money well spent on something that feeds your soul, and of course you deserve to be happy and enjoy your life.

4. End your meditation by committing to take the first step towards making your dream a reality. It may mean a phone call, doing research, signing up for a class or quitting your job. Whatever it is make sure you make the leap into your future and your happiness.

BAD HABITS

If you have bad habits that affect your mental, emotional, physical or spiritual health, this meditation will help you let go of them and start anew.

HEALING IS NOT JUST
FOR PHYSICAL ILLNESS.
TRY THIS WHEN YOU
ARE STRUGGLING WITH
NEGATIVE HABITS

1. Write down any negative habits you have had in the past or have presently. Take your time and be as thorough as possible. Then write down any feelings you have about your negative habits. Include any shame or regret.

2. Build a fire in your fireplace or barbecue. Sit on a meditation cushion or a chair nearby. Read your list. Review everything and feel your shame and regret.

3. Visualize your higher power in any form you like. Express your regret for indulging in negative habits and ask for help in living your life in a more positive and constructive way. Feel your higher power's love and acceptance of you as you are.

4. Now place your list into the fire and watch it burn. As your list burns, visualize your negative habits leaving you. Let go of any shame by mentally giving it to the fire to be purified. Commit to living a more positive life.

MEDITATION IS A WAY
TO CARE DEEPLY FOR
YOURSELF AND OTHERS.
IT AFFIRMS TO YOURSELF
THAT YOUR LIFE IS
IMPORTANT, PRECIOUS
AND FLEETING.

NO MATTER WHAT
BRINGS YOU TO
MEDITATION, OR WHAT
FORM YOU PRACTISE,
YOU WILL DEFINITELY
FIND IT WORTH YOUR
TIME